6 Figure Entrepreneur

Starting A Profitable Business Right Now

Maurice Sanders

TABLE OF CONTENTS

Introduction

Starting a business and becoming an entrepreneur will change your life for the better. The steps to becoming an entrepreneur have never been easier. The author has been through the fire, and has learned the hard way about the pitfalls of striking it out on your own. He's been through foreclosure, bankruptcy, divorce, job loss, business and money issues. The pages of this book will help you prevent the mistakes that I made. Maybe, your picking this book up because you've always wanted to go into business for yourself. But, aren't sure where to begin. Take the next 21 days to read the pages of this book, while taking action so that at the end of the next 21 days you'll:

Have a vision and a concrete plan for your business
Know what business you're going to start
Know your target market
Have a website
Have a social media channel
Have your business incorporated

Once those things are accomplished; you can take the next step to creating a business that returns $150,000 a year in revenue. A business that will allow you take control of your time and do things on your terms. The reason I know that all this is possible is because I've done it a couple of times. I've learned that the results will come if you put your head down and get to work. Will there be tough times? Yes, there will be. Will there be days when you want to give up? Yes, there will be. But at the end, you'll have accomplished something that will make you a better person.

Congratulations! Because you're on a journey that will change you forever!

Chapter 1: Small Business Basics

"Don't worry about being successful but work toward being significant, and the success will naturally follow."
- Oprah Winfrey

Starting a small business often means holding all the jobs in that business. Small businesses are a significant part of the economy of practically every nation. My first attempt at business was after watching the show Mr. Belvidere on ABC; on the show, one of the children in the house started a business where he'd take care of odd jobs for people in his neighborhood. The very next day, I handwrote some flyers. This was in 1987 before copy machines and printers were in just about every home. I went on a placed a flyer in every mailbox around my neighborhood. I didn't know that placing items in a mailbox was illegal. I didn't receive any customers from my initial prospecting efforts, and I quit! Fortunately, my perseverance has really improved since then. We'll talk more about determination in Chapter 8.

Generating a name for your company

Creating a name for your business is challenging, but it's an essential first step to take. It's usually easy because it's during the infatuation stage of your business. Just like in a new relationship, when you first start a business, all you can see is stars and dollar signs. As you mark the day, you tell your boss to take this job and shove it.

It requires brainstorming and picking at least four to five names for your business. That you then bounce those names off of close friends and associates for their feedback. Your business name must be unique and must not have been previously used as a business name by another company in your particular industry. Some names are registered across all sectors. This is the tactic used by Jay-Z and Beyoncé when they trademarked their oldest daughter's name Blue Ivy across numerous industries. This is rare. Checking the uniqueness of your brand name can be done by doing a U.S. Federal Trademark Search. This will confirm that another entity has not taken it.

Trademarking your name

It's simple and straightforward. A company that intends to register its name for a trademark can simply apply online. It takes less than 90 minutes and can be done with or without a lawyer's help. Disclaimer time: this book is simply for informational purposes only. Please consult a professional regarding your business needs. I've personally used online legal preparation services to handle the legal structures of all my entrepreneurial pursuits. The simplest and easiest way for people in the United States to register is on the U.S. Patent and Trademark Office's Website, www.uspto.gov.

Different types of business entities

What is a business entity?

A business entity is simply the structure of a business. It is an organization established by an individual or a group of individuals to handle transactions, engage in a trade, or partake in similar activities. One of the primary choices a business owner must make, along with his bookkeeper and legal advisor, is which business entity is best for his/her particular business—quick note on bookkeepers, accountants, and attorneys. Make them a part of your original success team. Otherwise, you'll end up like a particular author who lost hundreds of thousands of dollars due to his mismanagement. The hundreds of thousands are easily into the tens of millions in potential lost revenue due to lack of organization.

A business owner primary focus in choosing the proper business entity are:
(1) Responsibility;
(2) Clarity of agreement and activity;
(3) Taxes
(4) Suitability to business goals

There are various types of business entities. They include; sole proprietorship, partnership, I.e., general partnership, limited partnership (L.P.), limited liability company (LLC), and Private corporation, i.e., C-corporation and S-corporation. The type of business entity you choose will impact everything from funding and taxation to insurance and how the owner's demise will affect the company.

1. Sole Proprietorship.

A sole proprietorship entity saves money, time, and is relatively straight forward. All businesses default to sole proprietorship if no other business entity is created. While this may seem like the best way to start; but as Benjamin Franklin famously said:

"Pennywise; pound foolish."

This means that even if you save money at the beginning, you could also lose thousands over the long haul. This was the business entity I used when I started my car restoration business, Clean Classics. This business began when I was fresh out of college, and my manager gave me a ride to a business lunch in a 1985 Buick Lesabre. To me, the car was beautiful; it was just his grandmother's old gas guzzler to my manager. My eyes lit up! I asked him if he would sell it to me. He laughed and said ... "Suuure." And there it was, one of the greatest truths in life. One man's trash is another man's treasure. I bought the car for $500. I thought I was taking advantage of him, and he felt he was taken advantage of me. So, I thought if he didn't know the value of this car. There had to be other people just like him. Clean Classics lasted a few years. I learned a few more valuable lessons about business. We'll talk about that further in the 10 Best Pieces of Advice in Chapter 8.

In a sole proprietorship, one owner makes all the business decisions and earns all the profits. It's s an unincorporated business owned solely by one person. The owner is personally accountable for all of the company's debts and obligations—he or she has unlimited liability. The owner is also liable in case of a lawsuit. Let's do a quick case study. Jonathan had spent the first 20 years of his career selling real estate for a major corporation. Over that period, he built a great life for his family. His wife was a stay-at-home mom. His three children aged 3, 7, and 9 were in the best private schools in their well off neighborhood. But Jonathan always had the itch to start his own company. He figured if he could sell and rehab homes for his job. He could do it for himself. He found a home in his neighborhood that was underpriced and needed a little work. Due to his perfect credit rating, he secured the house for no money down, after some renovations. The home was immaculate, and the first weekend that it hit the market.

A potential buyer was walking down the stairs to the bedroom. They tripped and fell to their death. The prospective buyer's son sued Jonathan for negligence because they failed to secure the handrail of the stairs. In the town, the "billboard lawyer" won the lawsuit, and Jonathan lost his home, his life savings, his children, had to go to public school, and his wife left him. All this because he automatically entered into a sole proprietorship when he bought the home.

A sole proprietorship may be operated under any name, and it should register its trade name. It will have a Federal Identification Number, which may be, but is not required to be, the same as the sole proprietor's social security number. The timeframe of the sole proprietorship can be no longer than the life of the sole proprietor. All income and expenses from the sole proprietorship flow directly to the sole proprietor, but the liability does. The sole proprietor is personally accountable for all acts and omission and the actions of employees in the execution of their employee obligations. All properties, business and personal, of the sole proprietor are subject to his creditors' declarations. Because individuals can't protect themselves from their omission or purposeful acts, sole proprietorships are often suitable for an individual starting a service-based business without employees. The individual should obtain sufficient insurance to cover liabilities for an omission in providing service. The sole proprietorship allows the owner to loosen into the new business without substantial preliminary charges. We don't recommend a sole proprietorship when hiring employees, selling a product, or taking up contract liabilities.

Partnership

Unlike a sole proprietorship, a partnership is more sophisticated to set up and to run. It includes an understanding between at least two individuals carrying on a business and the end goal of making a benefit.

There are inherent benefits to a partnership:
- ➢ Pooling resources of the partners
- ➢ Recognizing the strengths of each partner
- ➢ Recognizing shortcomings of each partner

A great example of this would be when Andrew Carnegie hired Henry Frick to bring Carnegie Steel business to the next level. Carnegie was more of a people person; Frick, on the other hand, led with an iron fist. Initially, the duo was a huge success. That was until Frick's lack of care for the common man led to one of the worst tragedies in American history:

- ➢ The Homestead Strike of 1892
- ➢ The Johnstown Flood of 1889

Entering a partnership is like entering a marriage and ensuring that you and the partners can co-exist together. It's also essential to have an exit strategy; because even the best partnerships will eventually end.

Unless contrarily declared, in a partnership agreement, the partnership will be supervised by the partners. All partners have permission to administer the business in the name of and bind the organization. Provided that a company compels at least two partners, all partners must obtain a written partnership treaty that imposes how the partners will interact with the partnership. Partners generally transfer money or investments to the partnership in trade for a partnership interest. This is usually a tax-free trade at the time of donation. If the partners approve, fresh partners may enter the partnership by transferring money or assets, or an existing partner may trade all or a percentage of their partnership interest to the incoming partner. Partners, moreover, may obtain a partnership interest in trade for services. However, specific laws apply, and partners who execute the standard procedures of the partnership are not dealt with as partnership employees. Partners are responsible for self-employment taxes. Partnerships are pass-through entities. However, the company will have a tax identification number and must file tax returns. All income/losses flow through to the individual partners; to be documented on their tax returns. Although partners naturally are allocated profits and losses in agreement with their pro-rata share (i.e., two partners would usually share proceeds 50/50), partnerships have enormous flexibility. They may give rise to individual allocations of tax items, answerable to specific rules. In an overview, these businesses are naturally simple to create, and they contribute a considerable amount of economic and administration flexibility. Income is taxed in the same way as a sole proprietor. Still, partnerships also have the same disadvantage as a sole proprietor: the partners do not enjoy liability protection, and creditors may seize their assets.

Corporations
In contrast to sole ownerships and partnerships, corporations have a different legal presence separated from the enterprise's investors. Often called a Limited Company, an organization is a legal entity independent and unmistakable from its members (investors). Every investor's risk is limited to the amount of capital contributed. A lender with a case against the organization's assets would ordinarily have no rights against its investors.

The corporation has a structure different from sole proprietorships and partnerships. A corporation is generally managed by a Board of Directors, which must consist of no less than the lesser of three persons or the number of stockholders.

Ownership is divided into shares that are owned by stockholders. The stockholders of a corporation are those who have invested cash or other assets in acquiring an ownership interest (stock). As stockholders of the corporation, they are responsible for electing a Board of Directors and making decisions on significant corporate actions. Except in the case of a closed corporation, which we'll discuss later, stockholders manage the business. That job is left to the Board of Directors. No stockholder with less than 50% ownership can single handily bind the corporation to agreements or commitments. The stockholder's power comes solely in official action taken in meetings and by stockholder votes.

Corporate officers have general responsibilities for keeping the corporation in operation daily. The Board of Directors appoints the officers of a corporation. A corporation must have a president, secretary, and treasurer, but frequently corporations elect one or more vice presidents, assistant secretaries, and assistant treasurers. Other elected officers can include a chairman of the board, chief executive officer, chief operating officer, or chief financial officer.

Corporations can come in two forms:
- C corporation
- S corporation.

C Corporation
C corporations are subject to subchapter C of the internal revenue code. Unlike partnerships, corporations may have only one owner and can only be established by formally filing paperwork with the Secretary Of State. Rules for filing and nominal filing fees apply here. There are record-keeping and yearly reporting regulations. While we advise speaking with a lawyer and a tax professional when deciding on your specific legal entity. I made a huge mistake when I used a C corporation as the entity for my trucking business. I came to

this realization after I fell victim to double taxation to the tune of $60,000. The corporation was taxed for the revenue it earned, and I also incurred a personal tax bill as the corporation's primary owner. Two tax bills for the same income.

Here's a quick example of how I shot myself in the foot:

o John and Jane walk into Walmart, looking for a box of cereal.

o John picks up his box of cereal for $2.99 and heads to the register. John pays at the register and taxed 10% for a total of $3.28.

o Jane picks up her box of cereal for $2.99 and heads to the register. John pays at the register and taxed 10% for a total of $3.28. As she proceeds to leave the store, another cashier scans that same cereal box at an additional tax rate of 5% or 14 cents more in taxes, for a total of $3.42.

o John and Jane bought the same box of cereal, but Jane paid 14 cents more. Lack of knowledge can cost you in the short and long run. Fourteen cents sounds like a small amount. But when you talk about revenue, that goes from the hundreds of thousands to the hundreds of billions. It could mean the difference between profitability and bankruptcy.

S Corporation

The S Corporation is a variance of a C Corporation; it is governed by subchapter S of the Internal Revenue Code. Although an S corporation has practically all of the same C corporation factors, encompassing liability protection, S corporations are different in that they are taxed in a manner identical to partnerships. There are also constraints regarding ownership and restrictions regarding the allotment of income and distribution of company revenues.

A corporation remains valid until it is dissolved under state law. Both the corporation and shareholders will naturally possess tax effects upon liquidation.

Limited Liability Company

A Limited Liability Company (LLC) is a composite entity incorporating some of the best characteristics of corporations and partnerships. It is, practically, a partnership with limited liability coverage. The LLC limits liability for the business owners and a pass-through of the business's taxable income or losses to the owners. After my mistake with my trucking business, I made sure not to make that same mistake twice. Remember, one wrong decision is a mistake, repeating a bad decision in a choice. I formed my media business as an LLC.

Limited partnerships with general corporate partners can be utilized to obtain results similar to those proposed by an LLC. Such alliances can be overly sophisticated in configuration and policy for the business's objectives to be administered. Unlike Corporations, an LLC:

(i) does not restrict ownership to specific individuals,
(ii) is designed to allow pass-through taxation and individual allocations among owners, and
(iii) limits every owners' liability to the extent of their capital contributed to the business.

Back to the example of house flipper, when the fatal accident occurred in his renovated home. Had he bought the home under an LLC; the lady's estate could've only sued his company for the LLC value. In this example, the equity in the house. They could not have gone after his assets. As long as he managed the LLC as a separate entity; and didn't pierce the corporate veil.

Piercing the corporate veil or lifting the corporate veil is a legal decision to treat the rights or duties as the rights or liabilities of its shareholders. Usually, a corporation is a separate legal entity that is solely responsible for the debts it incurs and the sole beneficiary of the credit it is owed—for example, commingling business and personal assets like buying groceries for your home out of the LLC's bank account.

I've made this mistake several times; I struggle with organization. That is why it's crucial to have a good support system in place. Such as a bookkeeper or partner to keep you on track.

Pros and cons of each type of entity
Before initiating a business, one of the first essential things you do is decide on what your company's structure would be like, I.e., by selecting a business entity type.

Each entity has its Pros and Cons that you have to weigh before deciding on a specific course of action.

Sole proprietorship
Pros:

1. Losses from the business can balance income from different sources.

2. The board is concentrated since there is just a single lawful proprietor.

3. Record keeping might be somewhat easier.

4. It is easy to remove cash from the business.

Cons:

1. It is unlikely to secure income like other business entities.

2. The proprietor has no limited liability protection.

3. Continuity and transferability of interest are restricted

4. Certain tax deductions aren't allowed as with other business entities

Partnership
Pros:

1. If there is more than one proprietor, it is the more straightforward entity to set up

2. Losses can offset other income for the proprietors

Cons:

1. Limited liability protection does not exist.

2. A partnership may come to an end upon the cessation of the primary partnership interest. Therefore, continuity might be limited.

3. Profits must be kept in a business bank account, and tax-exempt incidental advantages are constrained.

Limited Liability Company
Pros:

1. This entity has a fraction of the better parts of a partnership combined with that of a corporation. Although it has limited liability protection, it considers the "flow-through income, so there is a lower possibility for double taxation.

2. It differs from the "Sub S" corporation, which places restrictions on the number of, and shareholders, and the sort and status of these investors. There is significantly more

flexible here. Salary and losses can be apportioned all the more effectively too.

Cons:

1. States have different rules and guidelines concerning their activity, lawful status, and limited liability protection level.

2. Also, similar to a general partnership, tax-exempt fringe benefits are limited. From a qualifying viewpoint on a governmental level, there is consistently the likelihood that the LLC will be tested on its capability. This could prompt circumstances where it is renamed as a partnership, and double taxation occurs

Corporations
Pros:

1. Limited liability protection to proprietors

2. Simple transferability of business license

3. Regardless of whether actual proprietors do not exist anymore, the business continues.

4. Estate planning for tax purposes is more straightforward.

5. Increasingly conceivable tax-exempt incidental advantage plans

6. Progressively adaptable annuity plans.

7. It takes into consideration different number of proprietors to make an interest.

Cons:

1. A corporation is increasingly troublesome and expensive to set up or end.

2. Substantially more planning is required to stay away from double taxation.

3. Record keeping can be confusing to limited liability.

4. Removing cash from the enterprise can likewise get dubious.

5. Finally, tax return filings must be particular.

Filing for your business entity

To protect yourself from liabilities and save your money from taxes forming a business entity is the simple way to achieve this. Here are the factors to consider before filing for a business entity:

1. Limitation of Liability

Liability insurance is one of the most vital advantages of establishing a business through an entity. The degree of coverage may differ; however, distinct entities give business owners the alternative to limit their liability. In other words, even though the business entity will be accountable for any debt, it incurs and administering a business using an entity can assist owners in protecting their assets from the company's obligations. Nonetheless, it is essential to note that this kind of liability insurance does not ensure the business itself from liability. Creditors will mostly be eligible to attain business assets. Moreover, the entity will mainly be responsible for any other liability that may occur in the business' conduct, like liability for accidents and injuries. Therefore, business insurance is always a significant element to have in place, regardless of the type of business entity.

2. Taxation

The essence and importance of taxes is another pivotal deliberation in choosing a business entity. Some entities are taxed, and may even give rise to double taxation (this means that both the business and the owners pay tax on business income). Others – so-called pass-through entities – are not taxed, and the business income flows through to the owners, who report their share of business income on their tax returns.

I learned this the hard way. It's best to invest the time and money with a good tax lawyer and accountant; to avoid losing your company's profitability or assets to the IRS.

3. Ownership and Management

Every category of business entity will have a different strategy of ownership and management problems to evaluate. Some entities invest considerable flexibility as to who can be an owner of the business. While others have stringent ownership regulations. Some entities have very detailed rules about how the company must allot income to the owners. While others mainly authorize the owners to distribute income as appropriate.

4. Authority and Business Formalities
Owners must embrace specific rules considering business authority, character, and system. Proprietors must understand that it is the entity that administers business, not the people who hold it.

5. Management of Capital
It is essential to assess the way money and assets will be arranged into the entity. Holders may donate cash or assets. The company may lend money that is essential to expansion or sustainability. Different entities have different rules that pertain to capitalization cases, particularly with concern to personal donations and loans from owners or third party lenders.

6. Transfer of Ownership and Estate Planning
Businesses have numerous options of ownership and laws that apply as to the transfer or sale of an ownership interest. These laws may influence how an owner trades an ownership interest to another owner or outsider. As well as specific laws that pertain to estate planning or a succession plan.

7. Filing it yourself

The key to choosing an entity is to recognize your objectives and look for guidance to figure out what type of entity will accomplish those goals. The conversion from one entity to another might be possible, but there might be adverse tax consequences related to such a change. Hence, it is ideal to give careful thought before deciding to guarantee that the entity you pick will address your issues. Choosing an entity should be made after careful thought and consideration.

Retaining a corporate law attorney

Getting a corporate law attorney largely depends on the type of business entity run by the business owner. In a business run by a sole proprietor, the sole owner can hire a corporate law attorney. If a company runs as a partnership, the question of who has the authority to appoint a corporate attorney comes in place.

Things To Remember

1. Getting a name for your brand is a necessary but difficult step. It is vital that you select a unique name to prevent trademark infringement.

2. Once you find a unique Name, trademark it immediately

3. There are different types of business entities, and specific steps are involved before filing one

4. You can register for an entity yourself, presenting the necessary documents.

5. Once you've decided on an entity, it's best to hire a competent corporate attorney to prevent legal issues.

Chapter 2: Entrepreneurial Mindset

"I learned to never kick someone when they're down.
Everyone makes mistakes, and some are real whoppers. But
that makes them whopping opportunities, too. "
— Jack Welsh

As an entrepreneur, you will be responsible for making sure all your business systems run smoothly. The most successful entrepreneurs are the most particular with their time and resources. The majority of small businesses do not intend to innovate or expand their operations but are instead content at their current size. It is up to you and your mindset to decide if you want to grow beyond your current level. You can be said to have fully grasped the entrepreneurial mindset when you become a serial entrepreneur. As inferred by the name, serial entrepreneurs create a career out of starting businesses. It's not required to start several companies to adopt the entrepreneurial mindset. It just means the entrepreneurship has become an addiction.

Characteristics of an entrepreneur

1. An entrepreneur views needs, issues, and challenges as new chances.
2. An entrepreneur thinks of inventive approaches to managing difficulties/issues.
3. An entrepreneur understands that he/she is in the business of solving problems\

4. An entrepreneur sees a problem before it arrives.

5. An entrepreneur is a visionary and a pioneer. As Jack Welch famously said, "Entrepreneurs see around corners for the next innovation."

6. An entrepreneur must be goal-driven.

7. An entrepreneurial mindset is the tendency to discover, evaluate, and exploit opportunities.

Should you be an entrepreneur

Before venturing into a business, it is essential to ask yourself the following questions:

✓ Are you ready for the ups and downs of an entrepreneurial lifestyle?

✓ Should you be an entrepreneur?

✓ What can you offer to the market?

Being an entrepreneur is not just about the name or being called an entrepreneur. It's about navigating the various challenges of being a lifestyle. Ensure you have all the entrepreneurship skills, like a professional quarterback who just threw an interception; or an NBA player who just missed five shots in a row. They have amnesia and will attempt that next throw or shoot that next shot—entrepreneur's need to forget about BUT LEARN from previous mistakes. Entrepreneurs do not allow mistakes to make them afraid to make that next step towards their goals.

Personality Types of Entrepreneurs

There are different types of personalities of entrepreneurs.

The Myers-Briggs Type Indicator (MBTI), created by Carl Jung, is an assessment tool that helps identify a person's entrepreneurial personality. Entrepreneurs should take this test to know which personality type they fall under. MBTI identified four pairs of personality preferences and sixteen personality types based on perception. These sixteen personality types are the ones grouped into four different pairs.

Certain traits of entrepreneurs are distinct from those found in the general population.

The four pairs of personality types are as follows:

1. ENTP, THE DEBATER
ENTPs are exceptionally knowledgeable, and they are fast thinkers. They want to know the details of every circumstance so that they understand the intricacies of their business. Due to their appetite for more information, they become outstanding entrepreneurs. They can come up with remedies to situations most people would never guess.

They are also extremely charismatic, enthusiastic, and sharp humor intrigues others around them. They can be fascinating and enlightening at the same time. They'll go to any lengths to find the solution to a problem. Challenges that entrepreneurs will face hardly faze an ENTP.

Notable entrepreneurs that are ENTPs:

➢ Steve Wozniak
➢ Stephen Colbert
➢ Billy Epperhart

2.ENFP, THE CAMPAIGNER:

ENFPs are cause acquainted. They share the ENTP's sight for odds but govern chiefly by attracting others to fight for their cause(s). Passionate, yet soft and approachable in person, the ENFP has a gift for noticing where people are a good fit for their enterprise – and placing where they would be happiest and most useful. It's unusual to see an ENFP in a CEO's chair, but you will find them spearheading ventures, especially in the creative areas. ENFPs are also fiercely self-sufficient, which feeds their appetite to be entrepreneurs as well.

Notable ENFPs:
➢ Julian Assange
➢ Walt Disney
➢ Will Smith

3. ESTJ, THE EXECUTIVE:

ESTJs are results-oriented. Although the ENTP and ENFP are primarily dreamer types, the ESTJ is less imaginative and more practical. They are the ones who get things done. Unlike the other Entrepreneur types, ESTJs dominate with their decision-making method, and making decisions comes naturally. It's not that ESTJs are inescapably power-hungry, it just makes sense for them to be in a position where they can make the tough decisions and keep everybody functioning effectively.

They are great leaders, and often tend to become presidents of the United States! It is always helpful that they never shy away from challenges.

Notable ESTJs:
- ➢ John D. Rockefeller
- ➢ Lyndon B. Johnson
- ➢ James Monroe

4. ESTP, THE ENTREPRENEUR:

ESTPs are an incredible combination of leisure and intellect. They leap before they look and remedy their mistakes as they move. Their compassion for risk is high, and they can always get themselves out of sticky problems even on the move.

ESTPs love to have fun, which means knowing about as many people as possible, and they assist the neighborhood by being the de facto social chair. The ESTP has been branded the "tycoon" by being able to negotiate agreements and host parties on their yacht.

Notable ESTPs:
- ➤ Winston Churchill
- ➤ Donald Trump
- ➤ Peter Schiff.

What businesses work best with different personality types
Different personality types have various businesses that work for them and the rate at which they make their income. Once you discover your entrepreneurial personality type, then choosing an industry that fits it will become easier.

Ten Best Business Growth Strategies

1. Provide Excellent Customer Service:
Excellent customer service is a big influencer to the growth of any business. Providing your customers with excellent services boosts your sales, but it is also to the long-term success of any business. It also helps promote your business. Nothing will put a business out of business faster than bad customer service. Excellent customer service includes meeting and surpassing

customer expectations, being helpful to the customers, being reliable, and getting in touch with you.

2. Focus on the lifetime value of a customer

A long-lasting relationship with a customer must be well built and maintained by a business owner. You should place significant attention on how to ensure the lifetime cooperation between you and your customers. Providing excellent customer service is one way to ensure this. Focusing on the lifetime value of a customer is a unique strategy to help your business grow

3. Remember the 80/20 rule

This rule is also known as the Pareto principle, and it is attributed to Italian economist Vilfredo Pareto. It is said to be one of the most valuable concepts to life and time management. It infers that 20 percent of activities done will account for 80 percent of results seen. Write out ten goals, then set aside and work on the two most important goals out of the ten. These are the goals that are the most important to you. This rule simply states that instead of focusing on all your ten targets at a time, focus on the two most important goals on the list the most, and it will work for you. The Pareto Principle also states that 80% of your sales will come from 20% of your customers or profits. Also, 80% of your problems are rooted in

20% of your customers. As well as 80% of your productivity will come from 20% of your staff.

4. Know what customers to keep and what customers to fire:
Certain customers should not be entertained by a business owner, no matter what. One caveat is that if you only have one customer and that customer is demanding. Think twice before firing your only customer.

5. Reinvest in your business
This is a significant point to keep in mind in any business venture. A successful businessperson does not pocket all of his profits. Learn to invest and reinvest in your business. This will ensure the longtime success of your business, but it is also an excellent business growth strategy.

6. Know your numbers (P/L statements)
Take note of your profit and loss statements and balance them. A good bookkeeper can help you with this.

7. Slow to hire; quick to fire
Do your due diligence before you decide to hire a new employee. Employees who are bad for business or perceived to have some dirty tricks which may affect the company should

be fired immediately. Being slow with this decision may be disastrous to the life of your business.

8. Referral business is the most profitable way to obtain a new customer/client
Keeping a good customer record will most likely boost your referral business. When you offer excellent service to your client or customer, this will make them happy and eager to recommend your company to a friend, family, or even a total stranger.

9. Stay up to date on industry changes
An entrepreneur must always be informed about changes going on in the industry. Knowing a lot about your business is not sufficient. You must know what's new and what to let go of. You must also keep in touch with your customers to understand their preferences and opinions about new developments. Do not be arrogant or assume you know it all. Communicate with people, surf the Internet. Things like this keep the business going.

10. Eliminate Entrepreneurial ADHD

By their very nature, entrepreneurs tend to have new business ideas daily. They're presented with an endless stream of great business ideas. Trying to run multiple businesses will probably mean you'll have two subpar businesses. Grow one company and then branch off into another business. I've personally ignored this rule, and it caused a lot of time and money to be wasted.

Ten Reasons Businesses Fail

Businesses fail for a large number of reasons. While the people around you cause some of these reasons, most of them are caused by the business owner. A business without a business plan or vision can end up failing at the beginning. A company with little or no capital for its long-term sustainability will stop running at some point. Businesses might take the wrong turn and end up falling for the following reasons.

1. Lack of capital

A crucial point to note before venturing into any business is capital. Lack of adequate capital will unavoidably lead to the downfall of a company before it even starts. Your capital must be sufficient, and in proportion to the type of business you intend to build.

2. Lack of vision

When a person lacks the intuition on how to run a business or such a person lacks an adequate vision of how a successful business may turn out to be, their business is likely to fail. A business owner must remain optimistic and visionary despite all odds, if for anything, for his business's success.

3. Fear

Fear can stop a person from achieving many things. All business ventures involve risks. A person who is afraid to take calculated risks is stunting the growth of their business. If you want to set up a successful business, let go of fear. Other than ambition and a touch of happenstance. Nothing is more prevalent in the life of an entrepreneur than fear and overcoming fear.

I learned that courage was not the absence of fear, but the triumph over it. The brave man is not he who does not feel afraid, but he who conquers that fear.
-Nelson Mandela

4. Poor execution

A lack of or a poorly executed business plan is likely to lead the business to failure. This crucial first step will help you plan for challenges. More importantly, it can keep you on track when the inevitable setbacks occur.

5. Working in the business and not on the business:

As confusing as this may sound, a business owner who spends more time working on the business's day-to-day operations will severely limit the business's growth potential. To push the wheel of an organization forward, one must be actively involved in all business tasks. But to take the company to the next level, one must continuously review the business's goals. Look at the expenses of the business and study industry trends. Hire staff that can carry out mundane tasks. The explosion of virtual assistants allows for inexpensive labor; that can return astonishing results. Time must be spent studying the competition. What are they doing that you can implement into your company?

6. Poor customer trafficking

Customer acquisition is the most expensive way to get a new customer. That's why it's vital to pay attention to the source of a new customer. This is why companies have the "How Did You Hear About Us" question when buying a product. Once you acquire a customer, you want to follow up with them via email, social media, or phone. To turn them into lifelong customers because once someone spends money with you once, they're exponentially more likely to buy from you again.

7. Entering industries that don't fit with your natural gifts

A person whose natural skillset is in mechanical services should be careful not to start a business related to that field. The one caveat to that is if a person is passionate about an industry that requires a new skill set is learned.

8. Burn out

After the initial honeymoon period of your business passes. The day to day grind starts. And you'll need to take time away to avoid losing momentum.

9. Quitting too soon

This is the most frequent mistake that causes new business owners to stumble. As a business owner, you are likely to experience challenges that make you question every decision that you've ever made. This is when it's essential to redirect and adjust your approach. I was on the verge of stopping my trucking company before it even got off the ground. I can remember looking for a regular job because things weren't as easy as I thought. Luckily, I stuck it out because a few months later, things took off. It is natural to get frustrated when things aren't going as planned. The most important thing is not to quit.

10. Lack of a support group/circle

This is generally important in life. Avoid the Debbie Downers and Negative Nick's of the world. They can steal your mojo in the blink of an eye. Avoid a group of friends that don't support you or your business ideas because keeping them around will unavoidably leave a negative mark on your business. Surround yourself with like-minded people, people with entrepreneurial mindsets, who will stop at nothing to achieve their goals. Limit your time with people who can't positively affect your business. The same goes for romantic partners. I've seen first-hand the difference between entrepreneurs who have spousal support and those who don't.

Ten Best Tips For Starting A Business

1. Do not be afraid to seek help: Always seek advice when you need it. No one, does it by themselves? As Tony Robbins has famously said, "Success leaves clues."

2. Seek advice from professionals who are competent in your industry: Seek advice from people who have done it before. Having a mentor will be beneficial, as well.

3. Keep a positive circle: Keep a circle of colleagues that will affect your business positively and supports your decision. Don't go about with people who have nothing but harmful advice to offer

4. Be ambitious: Let the drive be there. Don't get tired at the start- maintain that mindset that keeps you on your toes.

5. Calculate costs. Don't just assume any cost once you start developing your business. With every move you make, make sure you calculate the cost. Have a budget so you will not run into debt before your business starts.

6. Earn as you build. Don't focus on just building your business. Earn along with your progress. Don't just pour all your capital in without any returns. Earning will leave substantial and more capital to develop your business further.

7. Understand all the requirements for starting that particular business: Certain businesses require licenses or certifications to operate the business. When I had my trucking business, all drivers needed a Class A Commercial License. I also need insurance for all trucks and the cargo we would be delivering. As a real estate agent, I needed my salesperson's license. However, my media company didn't have any specific requirements.

8. Have a good idea about the general workings of the business:
You can rely on your own experience or have mentors or friends who have business experience. Like driving a car, the fundamentals of running a business are pretty much the same from one industry to the next.

9. Know what you are capable of and work on what you are not:

Know your strengths and weaknesses. One of the reasons that my car restoration went under in the early "00s is because I had a knack for finding a good deal. However, I had limited mechanical experience. I would purchase cars for cheap that needed extensive repairs. I would've been better paying a little more for cars that needed a few simple repairs or a paint job.

10. Be passionate and positive: Even if you bought a new car, it can't run on that new car smell. It needs gas to run. The same goes for a business. There will be moments that things aren't going as planned. However, long you think it'll take for your business to be profitable; double it. When times get tough, you'll need to remember your long term vision and why you started the company in the first place.

Things To Remember
1. Entrepreneurial mindset is what drives most entrepreneurs.
2. There are different personality types depending on the individual.
3. To know your personality type, you should take the MBTI test.

4. Due to the differences in entrepreneurial personality types, different businesses tend to work for different people

Chapter 3: Passive vs. Active Income Businesses

"Business opportunities are like buses, there's always another

one coming."

– Richard Branson, Founder of Virgin Group

Active income is like a dynamic salary that implies payment resulted from providing service and receiving compensation, wages, tips, pay rates, commissions, and pay. Examples of active income businesses I've been involved in were:

- Trucking
- Real Estate Salesperson
- Car Restoration

Primarily any service-based business where you get a direct return for time invested. For example, I would generate revenue in trucking per mile driven or loads delivered. Any income you gain by trading your time or skill for revenue is active income. A wage or salary would be an example of an active income. You're paid for every hour you spend doing something.

Passive income is an income stream from investments on properties, stocks, royalties, or shares. A passive income business is an income from investments. Passive income allows you to have more free time. Examples of passive income businesses I've been involved in are:

- ➤ Real Estate Investing
- ➤ Publishing

Passive doesn't mean no work is involved. It simply means there isn't a direct return for your efforts. For example, this book I'm writing requires writing, editing, publishing, and market the finished product. Let's say that it takes two months to complete the job and bring it to the market, with a total investment of let say $2,000. Once the book returns a $2,000 profit, any revenue earned after that point is an infinite return. This book can live on forever; the royalties it generates can pass on to my children.

Active income means a person is trading time to earn a direct profit. It's not a hands-off business. Some efforts of direct labor will lead to earning income. Passive income means you are receiving regular payment with little to no effort expected to keep it coming.

Pros of Passive Income

1. Passive income is usually generated by leveraging someone else's time, resources, skill sets, and unique abilities. This is why it is also called leveraged income.

2. It carries more tax-advantages than all types of income.

3. Passive income includes unearned income like pension, interests, unemployment benefits, and dividend payments. It

also includes rents, royalties, annuities, gains from certain foreign transactions, capital gains earned outside of business or trade, and income from the sale of a property.

Cons of Passive Income

It usually takes longer to receive income from a passive income business. You'll need special skills or have the cash to invest. Back to the book example, it can take years to recoup my initial investment. It's also harder to forecast income. With my trucking company, I knew that if I drove a certain number of miles or delivered a certain number of loads. I would receive an exact amount for my efforts. With my publishing business, things aren't as precise. There would be times when I thought I was on track and had created a proven system. Only for sales to fall off a cliff, a week later.

Pros of Active Income

You get a direct return for time invested. Income tends to be more predictable.

Cons of Active Income

There are limits to your income because there are only so many hours in a day.

Overlapping Businesses

Businesses can have components of both. I participate in day trading, but I also have long term holdings that generate dividend payment. I earn active income for my trading efforts and passive income from my dividend payments. With my trucking company, when I physically drove a truck, I was earning active income. When my drivers were driving for me, I was earning passive income.

Location Dependent vs. Location Independent Businesses

Determining the location is one of the business choices that must be made with care. The vast majority of location-dependent businesses have concentrated on the manufacturing sector, high innovation enterprises, and large organizations.

Choosing a location is a crucial consideration when beginning a business. While some industries are location-dependent, some can thrive regardless of their location. For example, a local food business will be best sold locally, as this is where the vast majority of their customers will be located. A change of location might be detrimental to the growth of the business. Therefore, before choosing a place for your business, you must first take a good look at the customer base. Here are a few things to consider before locating your business in a particular area:

1. Reception: how well your products will be received

2. Customer base: Are your customers at the location you are choosing?

3. Make inquiries about the kinds of product that is utilized most at that location

Online businesses

Over the last two decades, there has been a significant increase in internet users. Advantages of an online business:

1. Startup costs are lower than with a physical/offline business.
2. You can work with clients everywhere throughout the nation—or the world.
3. Customers value the comfort of getting to your business at any time of the day
4. You have the convenience to work from anywhere in the world

Disadvantages

1. Just 2 percent of guests to an Internet business webpage make purchases
2. More and more competition
3. Visitors have particular requirements for online merchants
4. Some clients may be less inclined to purchase. Added security and ease of use; has made online purchases relatively easy.

Things To Remember

1. People look at passive income skeptically because you do not work to get it, and it can be gained from investments, shares, pension, or rents.

2 Active income, on the other hand, is income earned from salaries, wages, or labor. Although it is said to be an enjoyable income, one of the disadvantages of active income is that it is heavily taxed.

3 There are certain factors to consider before choosing a location for your business.

4. Online businesses are less expensive compared to offline o traditional businesses.

Chapter 4: Writing Your Business Plan and Writing Business Goals

"Rule No. 1: Never lose money; rule No. 2: Don't forget rule

No. 1."

– Warren Buffett, CEO of Berkshire Hathaway

Having a business plan and goals is a crucial step in starting a business. A good business plan will help give your business a solid foundation.

Writing a Business Plan

A properly constructed business plan is the foundation of a profitable business. A sound business plan will act as a guide to starting and managing a business. It serves as the blueprint of your business—the underlying system that delivers this awareness of your entire operation.

A business plan allows you to review the merits of the business before a financial and personal allegiance to it. Your business plan will help you recognize and analyze your areas of strength and weakness. It points out business needs and business opportunities. That way, you'll notice problems before they escalate. This awareness and attention will help you accomplish your business goals promptly and effectively.

There are three reasons to establish a written business plan:

1. A business plan urges you to take a significant, and unemotional look at your business before and after its inception.

2. It is a governing tool that will assist you in overseeing your business and monitoring its progress or lack thereof.

3. It will express your ideas to others and provide the rationale for lenders; when looking to acquire funding.

Writing business goals

Writing your business goals leads you on the path to creating a vision for your company. Once you have a vision, you're more prone to stay on track towards achieving your goals. Goals and a vision will help you get through the tough times.

When things get tough

Even the most optimistic business owner should understand and almost expect hard that tough times are on the horizon. This mindset will give you the advantage to continually look for new strategies to help the business avoid future difficulties.

If a plan is working, there's no need to change it. Eighty percent of your time should be spent perfecting successful strategies, while 20% should be spent finding new ones. Multiple revenue streams will also help you manage tough times. Multiple streams of income don't require changing businesses. A company like Apple has over 30 different revenue streams.

Proper money management and using credit wisely will help you navigate challenging times as well. Businesses like real estate investing and trucking have excellent cash flow. To the point where the money it feels as though the income faucet will flow into perpetuity. But hard times eventually come. I've personally known dozens of entrepreneurs that have prosperous times and then out of nowhere BOOM; the steady supply of money evaporates. The lucky ones have family or friends help them get out of a tight jam. But for the rest of us, we're on our own.

I'm convinced that making money isn't the most challenging part of owning a business. The hardest part is managing a surplus of income. It's easy to understand why a company didn't succeed after a year or so. But when you have a thriving business for a handful of years, and you have to figure out why you don't have money when you run across a cash crunch. That's downright depressing.

A business might go bankrupt or have to face legal challenges for a reason or the other. It is vital to note this little mistake that creates a tough time for your business to avoid reoccurrence in the future. In summary, when your business is facing a difficult time, it's best to learn new methods and strategies that will create new opportunities for your business.

Business Ideas

Let's say you're struggling to think of what business to start. Here is a list of 25 ideas that can point you in the right direction.

- Furniture making
- Real estate agent
- Nutrition Coach
- Social media manager
- Freelance writer
- Vehicle service
- Life/ career coach
- Fitness Coach
- Photographer
- Modelling Agency
- Hairstylist
- Delivery service
- Home management
- Daycare/Babysitting Service
- Tutor
- Therapist
- Accountant
- Legal services
- Restaurant or Catering
- Self-Publishing
- Bakery

Things To Remember
1. A good business plan is the soul of any business
2. Write down your ideas and goals before starting a business
3. Remember to never give up when things get tough

Chapter 5: Best and Worst States For Business

"There are two types of people who will tell you that you cannot make a difference in this world: those who are afraid to try and those who are afraid you will succeed."
— Ray Goforth

Before incorporating your business, it is essential to consider the advantages of incorporating it in a particular state. A business owner must at least consider whether a state is business-friendly- some states do not create a business-friendly environment for business owners who intend to incorporate it. Nevada and Delaware are two of the best states to incorporate. The third state is Wyoming. These three states are favorable choices for incorporating your business because of their business-friendly rules, enhanced security, and competent courts. Understanding more about each of these states can help you bring about the best possible conclusions about your business and guarantee you get all the help you are looking for when you incorporate.

Getting your EIN

An EIN or Employer Identification Number is also known as Federal Employer Identification Number (FEIN) or the Federal Tax Identification Number. It is a unique number assigned to business entities for easy identification by the IRS. Essentially, it's the Social Security Number for the business. Whether or not they have employees, every business needs to have an EIN. Organizations shouldn't apply for an EIN if they are not legally formed. An organization applying for EIN must obtain Form SS-4, and it's instructions. An EIN can be purchased online, by mail, or by fax. In case the organization was formed outside the U.S. or U.S. territories, such an organization may also apply by telephone. Companies can charge over $100 to file for your company's EIN, but it can be obtained for free at IRS.gov.

Business insurance

The insurance coverage for business will differ depending on the industry the business is involved in. Getting protection is essential to cover unforeseen occasions, such as misfortune or harm to your property, legal cases, and environmental hazards. Getting the right business protection is a significant piece to setting up a legitimate and manageable business and limiting danger. Without it, you might not be able to exchange or have huge cash-based costs, leading to shutting your business down. It's crucial to define your type of business, and daily activities as these will affect the insurance cover types and categories you deserve. An insurance scheme that satisfies your business needs will ensure a span of unpredictable occurrences, like an office or factory fire, robbery, or storm destruction. Your sort of business and day by day exercises will decide the type of insurance required. From a money related viewpoint, it's essential to investigate the kinds of coverage needed so these expenses can be a part of your general financial plan.

I was at fault for being underinsured when one of my drivers for my trucking company got into an accident. Luckily the driver walked away without a scratch. The truck was underinsured, and I was forced to repair the truck instead of replacing it. The truck was never the same after the wreck.

Building Your Credit

Building your business credit can be a delicate step to take. Credit plays an essential role in the life of both the business and the business owner. Credit is used in the agreement to pay back for borrowed funds used in paying for goods and services bought with a loan. The sale of most commodities is facilitated through the extension of credit. Without a credit history, getting a loan, a credit card, or even an apartment may pose difficulties. However, you cannot get a payment or repayment without building credit first. Business credit can be established with or without a credit card.

A business owner that intends to build credit without a credit card might have to try a credit builder loan, secured loan, or co-signed loan. In summary, secured credit cards and credit loans can help build good business credit. The following are some of the ways a business credit can be built. There are two types of credit; personal credit and business credit. Responsibly establishing credit in a business can help achieve long-term dreams and goals. There are three types of credit tradelines; revolving credit, installment credit, and mortgages.

Personal Credit

Your personal credit might just be the alternative for a chance to finance the business. You should understand the risk and have the arrangement to create business credit and improve it to meet the company's necessities. Utilizing individual credit to finance your business can put your family and personal resources in danger. If the business comes up short or encounters a cash shortage, lenders can come after YOU, as you will be personally responsible for the company's debts. When one of my businesses fell on hard times; A business debt became my debt. That debt affected my credit score.

What is a FICO score?

A credit score is a 3-digit number used by a creditor to determine whether credit should be issued. FICO scores are the most utilized financial assessments. FICO is also the most commonly used method of scoring a personal loan. Each FICO score is a three-digit number determined from your credit reports' information at the three major credit bureaus—Experian, TransUnion, and Equifax. Your FICO scores predict if you are prone to take care of an acknowledged commitment as agreed. Creditors use FICO scores to rapidly, reliably, and equitably assess potential borrowers' credit hazards. FICO score is a numbering system established as a result of your creditworthiness premised on your previous and present credit usage. To know what your FICO score is, you should visit http://www.myfico.com.

What factors play a role in your credit score

There are certain factors to consider an individual's credit score. These are factors that can affect their credit score. The most crucial element of a credit score is to 'pay on time'

• The amount you owe is too high
• You owe too much on past-due accounts
• You owe too much on revolving accounts (i.e., credit cards)
• You owe too much on your installment accounts relative to the original amount
• You have a recent public record or collection on your credit report
•You don't have enough revolving accounts (i.e., credit cards).

I've had my ups and downs with my credit score. The origin of creditworthiness is trustworthiness. The less trustworthy you are, the more expensive financing will be; if you can get funding.

Three primary credit bureaus

There are three major credit bureaus of national prestige. These are Equifax, Experian, and TransUnion. These three significant bureaus dominate the market in obtaining, evaluating, and shelling information about clients in the credit markets. These are the three major bureaus that help monitor your credit score and reports. This primary agencies' main duties are to track how often a credit debtor pays back his money, whether he pays on time, what his total payments are, and anything else related to the debit account.

Most effective ways to build your credit

The most effective way to build credit is to start small and slow. This has proven to be an advantageous method to build your credit. It might be a little challenging to get your first line of credit or your first loan. Building good credit will result in improved cash flow, increased business loans or lines of credit, better terms with vendors, lower insurance premiums, and lower interest rates. The following are some of the most effective ways to build your credit scores.

How to recover from a bad credit history

It is essential to check your credit report because your credit score is a significant element that most businesses and banks that give loans consider when you request for a loan. Your credit score will determine your eligibility for any kind of loan and also specify the interest rate. Recovering from a bad credit caused by a blow from the past is not something that can overcome overnight. Maintaining good credit is vital if you intend to borrowing money in the future.

Maintaining a good credit score

Maintaining a good credit score is crucial to your business, as your credit score is essential to you. With excellent business credit, you can acquire the capital and credit extensions you have to develop your business and serve new clients. As previously mentioned, your credit score will determine your future possibilities of getting a new loan. Maintaining good credit scores comes with its merits, including getting a lower interest rate on your credit cards and loans. A good credit score lets you save money on insurance, security deposits, and bills. If an individual uses their credit wisely and responsibly, this will help them maintain a good score. Also, monitoring your credit reports is an excellent way to maintain your credit score. You must continually improve your business's credit score by monitoring your credit report and working with your partners and suppliers.

Things To Remember

1. Not every state is business-friendly, so you should be aware of a particular state's laws before incorporating it.

2. Getting Your EIN is vital to your business.

3. Business insurance is important

4, Credit is essential to your company, and building good credit history will help its growth.

5. Three major credit agencies monitor credit scores and reports.

Chapter 6: Business Banking

"The secret of success is to do the common thing uncommonly well."

— John D. Rockefeller Jr.

There are many banking services available to the entrepreneur. Banks often consider the small business sector as somewhat unattractive; because of high degrees of risk and little possibility for growth. They also feel this sector is expensive to operate. On the contrary, by enforcing the right business-standard, banks can adjust their relationship with small companies suitable for their risk model.

Opening a business bank account

Personal accounts and business accounts are open in entirely different ways. Before opening a business bank account, you need to write down your needs and how beneficial opening that bank would be to you. Observe the banks in your area. Schedule an appointment to discuss the needs and requirements of your bank. If the bank policy is not favorable with your type of business, you should try other banks to see which one suits your need the most. Take note of their customer service, accessibility, bank services, and costs. Inquire about the account types available in the bank to be sure you choose the correct product to meet your business's requirements. Look for banks that offer:

- ➤ No minimum account balances
- ➤ A vast atm network to cut down on surcharge fees
- ➤ Suitable loan packages (although having an account with a bank
- ➤ doesn't guarantee you can get a loan with that bank
- ➤ Suitable banking hours (including phone customer service hours)
- ➤ Low minimum opening business

Documentation needed to open a business account

You'll need the following documents when opening a business banking account:

1. Two forms of personal identification-- one needs to be issued by a government agency — for example, a driver's license or passport.

2. EIN, TIN, or FEIN -- Banks always require a business I.D. before they can open a business account. For sole proprietors, only the social security number is needed to open a business account, not an EIN.

3. Articles or certificates of incorporation

4. Business license; a business run by a sole proprietor must show a business license that displays both the name of the owner and its name.

Business documents depending on the business entity.

Depending on your business entity, take the original or a copy of one of the following documents issued by a government agency:

Sole Proprietorship documents

If the business name does not use the owner's legal first and last name, present one of the following:

• Fictitious Name Certificate or Statement
• Certificate of Assumed Name
• Business License
• Registration of Trade Name

Partnerships

General Partnership
• Partnership Agreement
• Fictitious Name Certificate or Statement
• Certificate of Assumed Name
• Business License

If you don't have one of the above and have not filed the appropriate documents, present a written statement signed by all partners implying that no documented Partnership Agreement exists. If you don't have documents administered by a government agency, then all lawful signers need to present in the branch when the account is opened.

Limited Partnership documents

- Certificate of Partnership
- Partnership document
- Statement of Qualification
- Partnership document
- Partnership Election

Limited Liability Company documents
- Articles of Organization
- Certificate of Organization• Certificate of Formation

Corporation
- Articles of Incorporation
- Certificate of Good Standing

Managing your business bank accounts

Effectively managing your business account is crucial to the success of your business. Most businesses entrust management responsibilities to an accountant or bookkeeper. Those who don't have the budget for an accountant may decide to manage their accounts themselves. They'll need to do the accounting yourself. Nothing will destroy a business faster than mishandling the business bank accounts. Abusing your accounts will lead to a business owner, not knowing where their money is going. It can lead to overdraft fees and returned checks. A primary factor that lenders look for is the number of overdraft and NSF fees an account has. You will be denied a loan based on this alone.

Keeping Personal and Business Income and Expense Separate

Experts recommend having a disparity between your personal and business finances, which will lead to accurate record-keeping. This will also help you understand your tax bill, an estimate of your annual corporate tax bill is due quarterly. Checks payable to a business must be written to the one named on that account. If you have to transfer assets to your account, the check should be payable to you. This creates a record of the movement.

Things To Remember
1. Banks overlook small businesses, but you can develop your business in a way that makes it look favorable to banks.
2. It is essential to open a business account for your business
3. Take notes of documents needed to open an account.
4. Employ the services of an accountant to manage your business accounts, and if you can't afford an accountant, you can manage it yourself.
5. It is vital to keep your business account separate from your account.

Chapter 7: Business Credit

"Successful people do what unsuccessful people are not willing to do. Don't wish it were easier; wish you were better."

— Jim Rohn

Like personal credit, there is also business credit, which also has a score associated with it. Your business credit can be one of the most critical factors in growing your business. Business credit records a business's financial obligation to determine if a company is reputable enough to lend money. Different agencies calculate business credit, and each of the agencies has a way of doing its analysis, but generally, this ranges from 0 to 100. A Paydex score measures business creditworthiness. A PayDex score is like the FICO score. While the FICO score is used to measure personal credit, PayDex scores measure business credit.

To check your business' Paydex score, you should visit http://www.dnb.com.The higher the number, the lower the calculated risk. The circumstances that influence business credit may include public records, like liens or bankruptcies, outstanding balances and payment habits, and demographic information, such as business size and years on record. Strong business credit can influence the growth of a business entity.

Here are only a couple of advantages of a strong business credit score.

1. It can help save some money. Lenders offer better financing costs to organizations with excellent credit.

2. You can acquire business credit without the requirement of a personal guarantee. This decreases your risk.

3. It can assist you in staying ahead of your competitors. You can pass your savings onto your clients.

4. You can settle on choices with certainty and get the cash you need.

5. Because of the importance of a business credit score, businesses are advised to establish a business credit report.

DUNS Number

DUNS means Data Universal Numbering System. Like the EIN, DUNS is a unique nine-digit identifier for business entities. The number is created by Dun & Bradstreet (D&B). It provides the name of a company, their phone number, address, number of workers, and open tradelines, along with other relevant corporate data. DUNS number can be applied free of charge from Dun & Bradstreet.

Using personal credit and personal guarantees to build business credit.

When handled responsibly, business credit can be used without a personal credit check. It can also be attained regardless of personal credit status. Most business credit can be obtained without the owner taking on personal liability or a personal guarantee. This means that, in case of default, the business owner's personal assets/credits can't be pursued. Without business credit, business is very much likely to suffer, not thrive. Building your business credit without your credit and personal guarantee will allow you to obtain more working capital. It will also allow you to borrow money at lower interest rates. Tax preparation is also simplified, and your credit is protected if your business ever gets into financial difficulty.

Ways to build your business credit

Nobody starts with excellent credit. They develop and build it, just like they do to their business. So, you don't have to be afraid to start little and work steadily towards the development of your business credit profile. The first way to build business credit is to register your business entity. To build credit, you should create a credit profile; and then take the following steps:

1. Open a separate business checking account. Use your business checking account to pay the business's bills and employees, including yourself.

2. Apply for and use a business credit card; this card will pay business expenses. Doing this will not only make monitoring expenses much easier, you'll also build credit for the business as you use and pay off the card. If you are not qualified for a business card immediately, start with a secured card backed by money you put into an account as collateral.

3. Ask for credit terms from your vendors. Even if the credit threshold is little to start, and the time frame is somewhat brief, it will help. Pay bills on time, and after a few transactions, ask to have the threshold increased. Success with even one or two vendors will give you positive credit references to build on with other businesses and for possible loans in the future.

4. Establishing or creating a relationship with your existing bank or another will allow you to seek their advice on the best type of financial product for your business need. It helps to build trust with a key vendor as your business grows or your needs change.

5. Register with the business credit bureaus like Experian and Equifax and open a business credit file.

6. Select your business structure carefully. The best way to separate your business and personal financial lives is to do it

legally. Instead of a sole proprietorship entity, form a corporation or LLC.

Things To Remember

1. Building good business credit is as important as building your business

2. Lenders will look at your credit score to decide whether or not to lend you anything.

3. DUNS number is essential and will be used as a means of identification for your business.

4. If possible, avoid using your credit and personal guarantee to build business credit

5. Ways to build your business credit include, opening a business account, creating a business profile, and applying for credit cards.

Chapter 8: Working With People

"No matter how brilliant your mind or strategy, if you're playing a solo game, you'll always lose out to a team." — Reid Hoffman

There's a wide range of staffing options, it is up to your business type and your preference to determine the types of employees you'd prefer to bring on board. People skill sets are required when it comes to working with others.

These include:
- ➤ Creating a good connection with others
- ➤ Strong listening skills
- ➤ Good communication,
- ➤ Team leadership
- ➤ Ability to negotiate

There is a unique skill in discovering what another person is trying to convey, and this can take many years to cultivate. It's also a skill to put people in the right places that fit their unique talents and abilities.

Types of Workers

There are three different types of workers. They include 1099s or independent contractors (also known as self-employed workers), W-2 employees, and Freelancers.

1099's and Independent Contractors

These types of workers are independent and self-employed. A 1099 employee is the same as an independent contractor. An Independent Contractor provides specific services according to the terms of a written contract. They may work on a project at a time or offer multiple services to different clients at the same time. The employer does not withhold any income taxes. The employer has limited control over an independent contractor's work.

W-2 Employees

A W-2 employee is primarily known as an employee. Unlike the Independent Contractors, a W-2 employee is a regular worker who receives regular wages and employee benefits. The employer withholds income taxes from the employee's paycheck. The employer also has a degree of control over the employee's work. The employer files an I-9 form on behalf of the employee; and used to deduct payroll taxes on a W2 employee.

Difference between Independent Contractors and W-2 Employees

The Internal Revenue Service looks at three things to assist in deciding whether a person is self-employed or an employee.

Those are:
> Conduct Control

> Money Related Control

> Relationship control.

Per the IRS, an employee falls under the following guidelines:

1. Your manager chooses when, where, and how you work. For instance, your manager instructs that you must be at an office consistently (or web-based) during essential business hours, equips you with a P.C. to carry out your responsibility, and lets you know precisely how to carry out your duties.

2. Your job chooses the amount to pay you, the amount of a raise, or reward you get and repays you for work-related costs. (This can be true for independent contractors as well)

3. Your manager gives benefits (like retirement and medical coverage) and expects you to remain with the organization until you resign or you're terminated.

A self-employed worker has a unique relationship with a company. A person is a 1099 worker when:

1. They get to choose when, where, and how they work with no imperatives (except in certain special cases).

2. They set their rates and pick whom they work with.

3. They don't have any benefits and have a predefined end-date

Freelancers

A freelancer is self-employed and offers services, often working on several jobs for multiple clients. A freelancer is similar to an independent contractor in terms of being self-employed. However, a freelancer can work with numerous clients simultaneously; an independent contractor mostly offers services to just one client at a time. Fiverr has a massive network of freelancers all across the world. I've personally used them for countless jobs for my media company.

The three types of workers can all perform the same tasks. Someone employs the fact that one worker is self-employed, and the other does not mean the services they will render is different. The only difference is the type of employment.

Difference between the independent contractor, freelancer, and employees

Although the IRS puts self-employed workers and freelancers are at identical tax rates, there is a significant disparity between the two types of workers. According to the Internal Revenue Service, a person is a self-employed worker when they're "in an independent exchange, business, or career in which they offer their services to the public."

The Internal Revenue Service records certain professions as examples of self-employed workers. Such as:
  ➤ Medical and Dental Specialists
  ➤ Legal Advisors

- Salespeople
- Temporary Employees

Be that as it may, a self-employed worker may also take on a couple of customers one after another. The business a self-employed worker acknowledges is typically long term. For instance, a temporary employee may be a carpenter, plumber, or electrician. You'll use their services for your home improvement needs.

Freelancers, on the other hand, work for as many customers as they can handle concurrently. Their tasks generally have a brief timeframe A freelancer may do one job at a time, or proceed onward to another business, or numerous companies.

Bringing People On Board

As a business owner, your hiring methods will lead to how others perceive you and your business. Your employees represent your company to customers, peers, and coworkers, and they may someday become leaders in your organization, so choose cautiously. It is not advisable to employ, hire, or go into contract with just anybody because you need someone's service. Before hiring a worker, expectations for the position must be clearly outlined.

Asking the right interview questions, and deciding on which person to employ can be a daunting challenge. A sound and productive recruitment process are crucial to your personal and business success.

You must employ people that set good examples of what your company represents while performing their job well. Reliable and competent workers are the most critical components of your business. A thorough study of applicants' backgrounds is necessary for the hiring process. You have to decide whether or not their personality and work ethic will fit your company. This requires much time spent studying job applicants, analyzing details submitted on resumes, communicating what they can bring to the company. Also, discussing what the company can do for you. Time invested in the hiring processes will save time in the long run to avoid onboarding a "bad hire."

Before you think of hiring a person, you must consider the following:
Hiring costs include the expenses of hiring a new employee, training them, and the learning curve that takes place until they're productive.

There is an adage -- Slow to hire, quick to fire! Choosing the right person for a job is important because hiring the wrong person can be exhausting. There have been several occasions where I've been quick to hire someone only to find out they had qualities that made them a bad fit from the position. Work ethic and a bad attitude are often the most significant issues when bringing on someone new.

You may find yourself under tremendous pressure to employ someone soon. However, the hiring process imposes a great deal of tolerance, mostly when you feel overworked or are anxious to expand your organization. Take the time to do it right, and you will be glad you did.

The hiring process requires a comprehensive recruitment process which includes:
- ➤ Hiring/Promoting from within
- ➤ Prospecting for potential employees
- ➤ Screening applicants

This usually includes posting a job ad with services like Craigslist or Indeed and asking for recommendations of friends, family members', and employees. The easiest step in screening applicants is eliminating them over the phone or with certain intricacies on the application. This will allow you to save time before bringing them in for a formal interview.

You'll need a thorough job description is an organized statement of the duties, with responsibilities and requirements of a specific job. Writing a description will enable you to manage your thoughts and articulate your hiring needs.

Larger companies follow a policy of expanding from within by widely disclosing all vacancies, empowering them with options for promotion. Hiring may result in crises if an outsider is selected; that's why it's crucial that you communicate with your staff that a particular position is open. What requirements are necessary and disclosing that you're also looking outside the organization, will prevent some of these problems. If you can't or choose not to promote from within, you have to seek out potential candidates.

The interviewing process is an opportunity for you and a prospective employer to learn more about each other; it allows you to go over the application or resume, asking questions, and assess the applicant's personality, character, verbal skills, and ability to navigate through challenging issues. The interview allows you to get a feel for the person instead of just reviewing an employment application.

Finding the best person to hire takes considerable time and effort. Screening candidates, digging through multiple resumes and applications, listening intently to what candidates have to say— and what they don't say—and deciding which person to hire is time-consuming and challenging. But consider it an investment in your company's future.

Things To Remember
1. Working with people is not easy, and it requires a set of skills like communication skills and leadership skills.

2. Hiring or contracting people for your business should be done patiently and carefully.
3. There are three main types of workers -- 1099s and independent contractors (self-employed workers), w-2 employees (wage earners), and freelancers (temporary workers).
4. The type of worker you hire depends on the kind of service you expect them to offer.
5. Take your time and patiently take the necessary steps, like the applicant's qualifications, before you hire.

Disclaimer: the content in these pages is for informational purposes only. Please contact a tax or legal professional before making any decisions. Remember to perform your due diligence before making any decisions*

About the Author

Maurice Sanders is a serial entrepreneur. He is an eternal optimist and has a knack for adventure. Having seen his fair share of ups and downs in life, he continues to develop businesses and jumpstart new ventures. He possesses a flair for teaching entrepreneur skills and has also taught at the Chicago Urban League.

Maurice holds a bachelor's degree in computer science and marketing from Northern Illinois University.

A couple of his favorite quotes include:

"Success is the progressive step towards a worthy goal"

"You will be the same person in five years as you are today except for the people you meet and the books you read"

When he is not working, he is sculpting or coaching new entrepreneurs into launching successful business ventures. He also enjoys travelling and thinking about his next journey in life.

If you're looking for help in reaching your life or business goals. Contact Maurice directly at maurice@mauricethefirst.com to invest in one on coaching. You can also follow us on Instagram @mauricethe1st. To get access to free resources to help grow your business while saving time and money visit http://www.mauricethefirst.com

Check out Maurice's other books:

6 Figure Trucking: You're Only One Decision Away From $150K
6 Figure Teens: Earn Six Figures Before Your 21st Birthday

To help us continue to bring the best books to the market. Please leave a review on the platform that you bought this book about what you gained from reading these pages. This also gives new readers the opportunity to see what knowledge other readers gained from this book

References

Business Concept; Wealth Creation & Passive Income

Business Entities: An Introduction, www.standardlife.ca

Business insurance a practical guide. Small Business Development Corporation, 133 140. usiness.wa.gov.au

CHOICE OF BUSINESS ENTITY

Business, Legal and Tax Implications; A Primer Presented for BALTIMORE COUNTY SMALL BUSINESS RESOURCE CENTER; White ford, Taylor & Preston L.L.P. © 2005 White ford, Taylor & Preston L.L.P.

Choosing the Right Business Entity; Phillip L. Kunkel, S. Scott Wick Attorneys, Gray Plant Moody, University of Minnesota extension

Credit score basics- Experian

Freelancer vs Employee vs Independent Contractor: What Are The Differences? By Rachel Pelta; www.flexjobs.com

Forming a Business Entity by Jane Haskins, Esq.by Jane Haskins, Esq; Freelance writer; legalzoom.com

Four Categories of Income www.smallbusiness.chron.com

THE FOUR PERSONALITY TYPES OF ENTREPRENEURS; wealth builders.org

How to Easily Build Business Credit without a Personal Guarantee: Kim Carpentier; Valley Credit Builders, G.M. Kim@ValleyCreditBuilders.com www.ValleyCreditBuilders.com

Introduction To Insurance By Cathy Pareto; http://www.investopedia.com/university/insurance/default.asp

Managing Your Business Credit, SBA

Personality Traits of Entrepreneurs: A Review of Recent Literature by Sari Pekkala Kerr, Wellesley College; William R. Kerr, Harvard Business School; Tina Xu, Wellesley College

Richard Brooks: HOW TO ESTABLISH BUSINESS CREDIT; Separating your personal And business finance

Setting up your business account : A simple guide to help you get started. Wells Fargo 2020

Small Business Basics, sony.com/yourDifference

Teaching the entrepreneurial mindsets to engineers; Bosman, L; Fernhaber. S; www.springer.com

The business of banking

The Keys to Successful Small Business Ownership, Finance and Credit™ National Foundation for Credit Counseling® (NFCC®) - Small Business Owner Counseling Program ;Client Workbook Version 6.0 ;March 26, 2018

Passive Income Vs. Active Income (A Beginner's Guide); he budget.com

Top 3 Best States to Incorporate a Business | LegalNature: www.legalnature.com/guides

Understanding Credit by Sallie Mae® and FICO - salliemae.com/FICO

Understanding Credit Scorecards: THE MODERN WAY TO AUTOMATE
CREDIT DECISIONS ON NEW ACCOUNTS AND TRANSFORM YOUR
BUISNESS, dun&bradsreeet
Understanding FICO score- FICO
10 Tips For Starting A Small Business That You Haven't Heard A Thousand Times
Already; Forbes.com

Made in the USA
Monee, IL
07 July 2026

56546310R00046